Palmer ★ Gibson
Ryan ★ Blue
by Dave Klein

GREAT PITCHERS SERIES 2

Revised Edition

tempo
books

GROSSET & DUNLAP, INC.
Publishers   New York

Contents

Bob Gibson   1
Jim Palmer   35
Vida Blue   55
Nolan Ryan   87
Statistics   109

Bob Gibson

Once again, in June of 1973, they said thirty-seven-year-old Bob Gibson was finished. His season record at the time showed five losses in his first seven decisions. As is his custom, however, Gibson battled back to win nine of his next fourteen. Not at all coincidentally, the Cardinals charged from last in the Eastern Division to first.

"With Gibby going strong," Joe Torre was to recall later, "I thought we were going to win it. He can pick a team up and carry it on his back. It's not only the victories, it's the way he makes things happen.

"During the second half of the season," Torre added, "you catch yourself looking ahead a little and figuring on Bob's starts as victories. When we lost him, it hurt in more ways than just statistics."

St. Louis lost Gibson—and probably the pennant—on August 4 at Shea Stadium when he twisted his right knee. He had been streaking back to first base to avoid a double play after a line drive had been hit.

Gibson refused help from stretcher bearers, and insisted on continuing. So manager Red Shoendienst waved relief pitcher Al Hrabosky back to the bullpen. But on Gibson's first attempt at a warm-up pitch, he collapsed again and had to be helped off the field.

Again, they said Gibson was finished. Too many injuries for a man of thirty-seven. Two broken legs and a long list of elbow and knee problems.

An operation was performed to repair torn cartilage outside Gibson's right knee, and as is his custom, Gibson proved a lot of people wrong. He returned to the mound on Septem-

4

ber 29. But it was too late for the young Cardinals to make a similar recovery.

Gibson finished up with one final victory for a 12-10 record as the Cards took second, despite losing twelve of their first thirteen games of the season.

For Gibson, the twelve victories represented his lowest total since 1960, when he won three of nine for St. Louis and two of five for Rochester in the International League.

"I've seen Bob win eight or ten in August and September alone," recalls Lou Brock on the theme of what might have been. . . . "Last year (1972) he started off 0-5 and won 19. He was just rolling along when we lost him. Not having his head around hurt almost as much as not having those good arms and legs."

Gibson, Brock (34), Torre (33) and Tim McCarver (31) are the "old heads" on the Cards and, while Gibson no longer enjoys the everyday baseball chit-chat with the press, he is not the sullen loner that some have painted him to be. He is intense, introspective and extremely articulate.

Just before his injury, Gibson talked about the value of having a group of veterans to help the young players. His statement tells a lot about the man:

"A team needs people like us (the veterans) not so much to teach the young guys about baseball as to teach them about life."

The "old guy," meanwhile, completed the 1973 season as the No. 2 strikeout pitcher in baseball history. Gibson moved past Denton Young and Jim Bunning with his 2,928 total. Only one man has ever passed 3,000. That was Walter Johnson with 3,508. And Gibson may even challenge that mark before he's finally through.

Gibson added one shutout in 1973 for a career total of 55, highest by an active major leaguer. Only Grover Alexander, Christy Mathewson, Warren Spahn and Pud Galvin have more.

Although Gibson did not reach his 1972 batting heights, he did belt a grand-slam homer in '73 to give the Mets a 13-1 pasting. The all-round athlete hit two homers for the season to boost his career total to 24 (not including two in World Series play), the most by an active pitcher.

Gibson hit five home runs in 1972, helping his own 19-1 surge on the mound. In eight starts prior to his first 1972 victory (May 25), the 6-1, 195-pounder received only twelve runs worth of support, and five of them came in one game. But Gibson does not hit by necessity alone. He is a superb athlete who might have been just as big a star as an outfielder or a first-baseman.

Gibson's 2.46 éarned run average for 1972 was his lowest since 1969 and he allowed only 14 home runs in two hundred and seventy-eight innings. On June 21, 1972, he beat the San Diego Padres, 14-3, for his two hundred and eleventh victory as a Cardinal, breaking Jesse Haines' career record.

Although Gibson had been a truly outstanding pitcher for at least five years before the 1968 season, he attained true stardom in that year. National attention finally came his way in the 1968 World Series between the Detroit Tigers and the St. Louis Cardinals. Seldom had any game been as eagerly anticipated as the opener on October 2.

Million of fans were filled with excitement at the prospects of a duel between the two starting pitchers—Denny McLain, Detroit's thirty-one-game winner and the recipient of the American League's Cy Young Award, and

Bob Gibson, St. Louis' twenty-two-game winner and recipient of the National League's Cy Young Award.

They had been, unquestionably, the two best pitchers in baseball during the just-concluded season, and as such they were the natural selections as World Series starters.

That year, McLain had become the first man to cross the thirty-game threshhold since 1931, and his daily exploits from the moment it seemed he might make it had been recorded by more newsmen and television interviewers than had ever seen the Tigers before. It had been a once-in-a-lifetime performance, and McLain was the reason the Tigers were favored to win not only this opening game but the entire Series as well.

Gibson, a tall, lanky, fireballing right-hander, had enjoyed a spectacular season of his own, one that included fifteen straight victories and five straight shutouts. But his record of 22-9 did not carry with it the inherent glamor of McLain's Miracle; hence, when compared to the Detroit star, Gibson's impact as well as his chances of victory seemed to pale.

It started out exactly as the fans would have expected, and for the first three innings both men were nearly untouchable. No runs crossed the plate for either team. The tension in the air pyramided to rarely achieved levels of drama.

But then, in the fourth, one of the pitchers cracked. And it wasn't Gibson. The Cardinals broke through against McLain to score three times, on two walks, two singles and an error. McLain had faltered, and the crowd of more than 50,000 in new Busch Stadium roared its hometown pleasure.

Gibson was still strong, still firing his frightening fastball, and now, because of the unexpected lead, more confident than ever.

By the sixth, McLain was gone, having been removed for a pinch hitter. The score was still 3-0. Gibson was getting stronger.

The Tigers tried, but they got nowhere. Almost unnoticed, Gibson began accumulating strikeouts, until after eight innings his total stood at fourteen. Today he insists he was totally unaware of his impending shot at the World Series record of fifteen set by Sandy Koufax in 1963; if so, he must have been the only one in the stadium who wasn't.

Entering the ninth inning, the Cardinals held a 4-0 lead, the fourth run courtesy of outfielder Lou Brock's home run in the seventh off relief pitcher Pat Dobson. Now it was Gibson against the middle third of the Tigers' batting order, the strongest, most explosive three men in the lineup.

First up was outfielder Mickey Stanley, and he drove a single over the infield for the fifth, and final, hit off Gibson that day.

With a man on first, up stepped outfielder Al Kaline, the Tigers' legendary slugger, one of the most feared, and prolific, hitters in the game. Gibson struck him out. Koufax's record had been equaled.

He had two more chances now, two more outs to get, two tries at setting his new record. First baseman Norm Cash glared back from the batter's box. The powerful home-run hitter had already struck out twice, but he took the bite on a rising fastball and went down for the third time, giving Gibson the World Series record.

Behind him, the huge scoreboard in centerfield lit up with a jubilant message: SIXTEEN STRIKEOUTS. The crowd broke into cheers.

The final batter, muscular outfielder Willie Horton, proved to be merely icing on Bob's cake. Horton struck out, making it seventeen

for Gibson . . . giving him the 4-0 victory . . .
giving him his sixth consecutive World Series
triumph . . . giving the Cardinals the all-
important first game. Gibson was half carried,
half dragged off the field by his catcher, Tim
McCarver, and other members of the elated
team.

"I really, really didn't know about the
strikeouts," he said later in the madhouse of
the St. Louis dressing room. "When I got
Cash, I was shocked at the noise the crowd
made. Then I turned and saw the scoreboard,
and I knew what it meant. I can't really put
into words the satisfaction I felt, but it was
partly because I knew we were going to win
the game. The World Series is the most important thing in baseball, and winning a game
in it is the ultimate a pitcher can achieve."

Gibson had already reached the ultimate.
The 1967 World Series, in which the Cardinals
had beaten the Boston Red Sox, had been Gibson's Series, completely. He had won three
games for the Cardinals, been named the Most
Valuable Player of the Series, had won the
new automobile presented annually by *Sport*
magazine, and had rested on top of the baseball world.

The opening game in 1967 was a six-hit, ten-strikeout effort. Gibson won the fourth game with a five-hit shutout in which he picked up six more strikeouts. And he had clinched it for the Cardinals in the seventh game, twirling a masterful three-hitter and adding ten additional strikeouts to his record.

A few weeks after that, Bob and his family received an invitation to dinner from Lyndon Johnson, President of the United States. "I'm not usually impressed by things," says the laconic Gibson, "but that got to me. Imagine, a poor black kid from Omaha, Nebraska, sitting down to dinner with the President in the White House. Just imagine that."

It had, indeed, been a hard road for Bob Gibson. And even today, Gibson is not totally without scars from his boyhood of poverty and prejudice.

Robert Gibson was born on November 9, 1935, in Omaha, the youngest of seven children. His father had died three months prior to his birth, leaving his mother to support the family on her meager wages as a laundress.

The Gibsons lived in a four-room wooden shack on Omaha's North Side, a ghetto area. They knew hunger and deprivation, loneliness and hardship, prejudice and sickness. Bob remembers that rats used to bite him at night.

"My mother was determined to keep us all together," he said. "She went without new shoes so we could have them. She wore the same coat for a third or fourth winter so we could have new ones. She always made sure we had food on the table. We didn't have much, but we had a real family spirit. It made up for a lot of things we lacked. I can remember putting cardboard in my shoes on rainy days so the water wouldn't seep through. I remember wearing my older brothers' clothes because we couldn't buy new ones. But I'll always remember my childhood with happiness, because of my mother."

His oldest brother, Josh, was Bob's substitute father. He kept the youngster on the right road. He fanned his interest in sports, and advised him to continue his education, not to fall victim to the temptation of the streets. "Sure, I could have gone the other way, and I would have gotten into plenty of trouble," Bob admits. "But Josh just wouldn't let that happen."

Josh, whose real name is LeRoy, was the oldest of the seven Gibson children and a full fifteen years older than Bob. He had experienced prejudice first, and had tried to shield Bob from it. But that is, and was, impossible. Josh, in fact, held a master's degree in history, but when he was discharged from the United States Army the only job he could find was that of a worker in a packing house. He wanted to teach and coach in high school, but the color of his skin prevented him.

Instead, Josh devoted his spare time to coaching basketball and baseball at the local YMCA, and it was there that he took young Bob under his wing.

"I played for the 'Y' teams and I can remember Josh working me harder than any of the other kids. I think back now and smile, but at the time I thought it was because he was picking on me. All the while he was trying to make me a better athlete because I was his brother."

Young Bob excelled in two sports, baseball and basketball. Josh counseled him to stay away from football, because as a boy he was not overly tall or heavy, and the higher risk of injury in football, Josh felt, might wipe out participation in any sport. Today Bob is 6-2 and weighs 195, but he didn't fill out until his late teens.

By the time Bob entered Omaha Technical High School, he was accomplished in baseball and basketball. But he did not get the chance to play high-school baseball, and he thinks he knows why.

"I reported for tryouts one day but the coach told me it was too late," Gibson remembers. "He told me to go play for the North Side teams, meaning the Negro teams in the ghetto." Gibson, who has never pulled punches, recalls in his autobiography, *From Ghetto To Glory*, that there were no Negroes on the high-school baseball team despite the fact that half the school's population was black.

A special satisfaction came later, Bob adds, when his 'Y' team, the Monarchs, won the Nebraska State 'Y' Baseball Tournament by beating a team coached by his high-school coach and composed mainly of those white players who were members of the school squad.

But basketball was a different story at Tech High. Four of the five starters were black, and Bob Gibson was the best of them all. He attracted considerable attention and several colleges and universities began to show interest.

Bob was dazzled, because his boyhood dream had been to attend college.

On the other hand, he had already received an offer to play for the Kansas City Monarchs, one of the most famous teams in the then-numerous Negro baseball leagues. "I was tempted to take it and start earning some money," Bob says, "but Josh wouldn't hear of it. He insisted that as long as I had a chance to go to college I should. But we had no money and I didn't have a job, and we both knew I would have to get a basketball scholarship if I was going to make it. We answered several schools, but I really had my heart set on Indiana University. They always had good basketball teams there and it was a good school. So my high-school coach, Neal Mosser, sent in a recommendation, and then we waited. Finally he got the letter. I'll never forget what it said.

" 'Your request for an athletic scholarship for Robert Gibson has been denied because we already have filled our quota of Negroes.'

"I just couldn't believe it. I came close to dropping the whole idea of college. But then Josh talked to a friend of his, Duce Belford, who was the athletic director at Creighton right in Omaha. Duce came back in a day or so with a basketball scholarship. I was accepted. It was a happy day for my mother, I'll tell you that."

Bob became a standout basketball player at Creighton, good enough to earn Honorable Mention on several All-America teams in his senior year. But he had to keep working to supplement the family's income, putting in time at a filling station from midnight to 7 A.M. He managed to keep his grades up, too.

As a basketball player, he established most of the rebounding records at Creighton, which stood until Paul Silas came along. Silas now plays professionally in the National Basketball Association.

Baseball was a collegiate pursuit of Gibson's, too, and he was both a slugging, switch-hitting outfielder and a pitcher with an overpowering fastball.

Finally, the Harlem Globetrotters offered him a contract with their touring basketball team, and the St. Louis Cardinals wanted to sign him to a baseball contract.

Bob managed to accept *both* offers. He signed with the Omaha Cardinals, a St. Louis affiliate, for a $1,000 bonus and $3,000 in salary for the season, and when the season ended he played for the Globetrotters for $1,000 a month on a four-month arrangement.

As a result, Bob earned $8,000 in his first year out of college. It was more money than anyone in the Gibson family had ever made in one year.

The first few years of Bob's baseball career were hardly distinctive, and there was little to indicate the staggering success he would later find. In 1957, his first year in organized baseball, he alternated between the Omaha Cardinals and a farm team in Columbus, Ga., in the South Atlantic League. He compiled a combined record of 6-4, with 49 strikeouts in 85 innings. But he was wild, and unschooled in the craft of pitching.

"I was a thrower, not a pitcher," he says. "I didn't have the faintest idea of what to do, except throw as hard as I could."

His performance did not improve dramatically in 1958, either, as Bob split his time between Omaha and the Rochester Red Wings of the International League. He ended that season with an 8-9 record, but was still not considered an immediate possibility by the Cardinals' management.

Then in 1959, he got the chance to stay with

one team—Omaha—all season. It made for improvement, and his season ended with a 9-9 record, and 75 strikeouts in 135 innings. Moreover, he had begun to master a curveball and a slider as additional pitches.

Now the Cardinals began to show interest. First they asked him to stop playing basketball in the winter months and offered to make up the salary he would lose. Then they brought him up to the major-league roster at the end of the 1959 season. He appeared in seventy-six innings and established a mediocre 3-5 record. In 1960, he was 3-6 for the Cardinals. Around mid-season, he was shipped down to Rochester.

Part of the problem in those years was Gibson's inability to communicate with the Cardinals' manager, Solly Hemus. Hemus had been a major-league infielder for eleven years, a fact which does not testify to his ability as much as to his determination and hustle. He was, at best, an ordinary player. "He was tough and combative," says Bob, "and he seemed to always carry a chip on his shoulder. I guess he didn't have time to work with young kids. I was tight all the time, and when I got a chance to pitch, he'd pull me out the first time I threw a bad pitch. He had me pressing all the time, the whole team, too. I just couldn't play like that. He made us all nervous."

July 6, 1961, then, stands out in Gibson's mind as what he calls Independence Day. The Cardinals, who had gotten off to a dismal start, fired Hemus and named the late Johnny Keane as his successor. Keane, a warm, friendly, affable man, had managed Gibson at Omaha. He later resigned after winning the World Series in 1964 and served as manager of the New York Yankees for just over a year.

"He was a fair man," Gibson said. "He cared about his players and he never would bawl you out in front of others, which Hemus did. He had patience with the younger men, too."

When Keane arrived in St. Louis, he took Gibson aside and spoke to him at length. "Hoot," he said, using a nickname he had stuck on Bob in Omaha, "you're pitching to-night and you're in the regular rotation now. Don't let me down."

The Cardinals rallied somewhat under Keane and finished the 1961 season in a tie for fifth place. But Gibson found himself a major-league pitcher. He had a 13-12 record with a 3.24 ERA, and although he still had a wildness problem (he led the league with his 119 walks) he began making inroads as a strikeout artist as well. He fanned 166 men in his 211 innings that season.

"It was like night and day," he says, referring to the replacing of Hemus with Keane. "I began to enjoy baseball again, and I thought we really had a good team, a team capable of winning a pennant in another year or so."

In 1962, Gibson added another pitch to his arsenal—a second fastball. "I was fooling around one day late in the sixty-one season," he says, "and I discovered that if I held the ball differently on the fastball delivery, I could make it do different things. Finally, I arrived at two fastballs. One I hold across the seams, and it sails away from a righthanded hitter. The other I hold with the seams, and it tends to sink into a righthanded hitter. It was really important, because it gave me an extra pitch. The fastball that sails away is my strikeout pitch. But when I have to get a man to hit the ball on the ground, like when we have to make a doubleplay, I use the sinking fastball."

The added pitch began to show in Bob's performance. In 1962 he won fifteen, lost thirteen and compiled an excellent 2.85 ERA. It also was his first excursion past the two-hundred strikeout mark in a season, as he whiffed 208 batters.

Things kept improving in 1963, when Bob became the ace of the staff with his 18-9 record, 204 strikeouts, 3.39 ERA and 255 innings worked. "We were close all season," he says, "and we could have won the pennant if I had won a few more games." As it turned out, the Cardinals finished second to the Los Angeles Dodgers, six games away, and watched as the Dodgers swept the Yankees in the World Series in four embarrassingly easy games.

The 1964 season was one that will remain in the minds of many people, but especially in those of the Cardinals and the Philadelphia Phillies, who reached new depths of futility.

On the fifteenth of August, Gibson was struggling along with a 10-10 record and St. Louis was almost ten games behind the league-leading Phillies. On the twenty-second, the Cardinals were fourth, eleven games behind Philadelphia with just thirty-nine games left in the schedule.

But the Cards kept winning, and Gibson continued to get stronger. At the same time, the Phillies began to falter. The suspense slowly mounted. With eleven games left to play, the Cardinals opened a five-game series with the powerful Pittsburgh Pirates, while the Phillies had a four-game set with an expansion team, the Milwaukee Brewers. Gibson admits he and his teammates were thinking about a second-place finish, not at all considering the unlikely possibility of a pennant.

But the improbable happened. St. Louis swept its five-game series against the Pirates while the frantic Phillies lost four straight.

Suddenly there was a pennant race. The Phillies were coming into St. Louis for a three-game showdown, and they had slipped out of first place, a game behind the hard-charging Cincinnati Reds and half a game ahead of the third-place Cardinals. On that day, the team records showed this kind of a race:

Cincinnati, 91-66.
Philadelphia, 90-67.
St. Louis, 89-67.

It all worked out for St. Louis. The Cardinals won all three games from the Phillies, extending the latter team's catastrophic losing streak to ten games, while the Pirates won two of three against Cincinnati. With three games left in the season, the Cardinals were

92-67, half a game ahead of the Reds and two-and-a-half ahead of the fading Phillies.

To make matters even more rosy, the final three games for the Cardinals were to be played at home against the hopeless, tenth-place New York Mets. What could go wrong?

"A victory over the Mets was all we needed," says Gibson with a wry smile. "I started the first game of that series and we lost, 1-0. Imagine. The Mets had been something like forty games out of first place and we had beaten them easily all season. Then they suddenly turned on us. And the Phillies turned around and beat Cincinnati."

The Reds and Phillies were idle the next day, but the Cardinals played the Mets again. And New York did it again, staggering the Cardinals by the score of 15-5. As a result, Cincinnati moved into a tie for the lead with St. Louis, with Philadelphia close enough to force a potential three-way tie.

It was the final day of the season.

The Mets moved in front, 3-2, and the telephone in the St. Louis bullpen rang.

"I had been down there warming up," Gibson says. "I figured I had all winter to rest if we lost again, and I thought if we got in trouble I might be able to help. So I was pitching and suddenly it was Johnny Keane, asking if I was ready. Sure I was. So I went in as a relief pitcher, for the first time that season."

The Cardinals scored three times in the bottom of the fifth, to take a 5-3 lead, and ultimately won by a ludicrous 11-5. Meanwhile, the Phillies were beating the Reds, 10-0. The Cardinals were National League champions for the first time in eighteen years.

Gibson earned the victory that day, his nineteenth of the year. He could have had his first twenty-game season but for a disagreement in May, when he argued with an umpire long enough to be ejected in the fourth inning while ahead, 7-1. He left one inning short of the required length of time a pitcher must go as a starter to receive credit for a victory.

"It would have been nice to win twenty, but it couldn't have been as important as us winning the pennant. What a great race it had been, and greater for us, because we won."

Gibson won two of three decisions against the Yankees in the 1964 World Series, a Series the Cardinals were to win in seven games. He lost the second game but came back to win the fifth in Yankee Stadium in ten innings, having allowed the Yankees to make up a 2-0 deficit in their ninth inning to send the game into overtime.

In the seventh and deciding game, he hooked up with New York's Mel Stottlemyre and won, striking out nine in the 7-5 victory. He had given up ninth-inning homers to Phil Linz and Clete Boyer, but Keane said he did not want to take his star pitcher out. "I wanted him to finish it. He deserved it. He had been just magnificent all season. I committed myself to his heart. I knew he would do it."

Gibson was acclaimed as the Most Valuable Player in the Series, and his season had been a completely satisfying one. But then Keane suddenly announced his resignation. It had stemmed from a mid-season change in the front office, when Bing Devine was dismissed as general manager and Bob Howsam named to replace him. The Cardinals were floundering then, and Howsam, feeling it was time to change the manager, was said to have offered the job to Leo Durocher.

Then, to Howsam's chagrin, the Cardinals put on their spirited finish and won the pennant and the World Series.

Keane quit on principle. He was that kind of a man.

"I'll miss him," Gibson said when he heard the news. "That man has done as much for my career as anyone."

The seasons of 1965 and 1966 were so-so for the Cardinals but lusty for Bob Gibson, as he put together back-to-back records of 20-12 and 21-12, striking out 270 and 225, respectively.

Then in 1967, when the Cardinals righted themselves and once more became terrors of the National League, Gibson was forced to sit idly by for much of the season with a broken leg. He had been struck on the right shin by a line drive off the bat of Pittsburgh's Roberto Clemente on July 15, and after pitching the rest of the inning, he collapsed in pain on the dugout bench. He was rushed to a hospital, where X-rays revealed the broken bone.

He had a 10-6 record at the time of his injury, and did not rejoin the team until September, when he beat the New York Mets, 9-2. He finished the season with a 13-7 record, but the Cardinals were easy pennant winners with such pitchers as Dick Hughes (16-6), Nelson Briles (14-5), and Steve Carlton (14-9) taking up Gibson's slack.

The 1967 World Series was against the Boston Red Sox, and despite having missed so much of the season, Gibson drew the starting assignment. Said manager Red Schoendienst on the eve of the opener: "If you have a man with the courage and ability of Bob Gibson on your team, you have no choice but to give him the toughest job."

Gibson won it, 2-1, beating Jose Santiago with a six-hitter, striking out ten Red Sox batters in the bargain.

Gibson made it two-for-two (and four straight World Series wins) in the fourth game, shutting out the Red Sox, 6-0, with a five-hitter. He added six more strikeouts. But Boston battled back to win the fifth and sixth games, forcing the Series to its final battle, and again it was Gibson who came up with the crucial victory.

He limited the Red Sox to three hits, struck out ten and clinched the Series with just three days rest. In his three appearances, he had allowed just fourteen hits in twenty-seven innings, tying a record set way back in 1905 by Christy Mathewson of the New York Giants. He also became only the seventh pitcher to win three games in one World Series.

There was no doubt as to the Series MVP. It was Bob Gibson.

Bob came back with another super season in 1968, at one point registering five straight shutouts. Then, however, he gave up two singles and a wild pitch, which prevented him from breaking Don Drysdale's brand-new record of fifty-eight and two-thirds scoreless innings. It was in a game against Drysdale, the Dodgers' towering righthander, that Gibson give up the run, but he won the game, 5-1, and established an incredible statistic of having allowed only three runs in his last 100 innings pitched.

Gibson was to win fifteen straight games during the season, winding up with a 22-9 record and a league-leading 268 strikeouts. In addition, he set a National League record with his amazing 1.12 ERA.

He led the league with thirteen shutouts and finished twenty-eight of the thirty-four games he started. Not only did he win the Cy Young Award, but he was named the Most Valuable Player in the league as well, a rarity for a pitcher.

That season set up the classic confrontation of the opening game of the World Series against McLain, when he struck out seventeen Tigers. He went on to win a second game in the Series, the fourth, with a five-hitter and ten more strikeouts. The victory was his seventh in a row in World Series competition, which still stands as a record.

But Bob lost the seventh and decisive game, 4-1, as Detroit capped an emotional rally by bouncing back from a do-or-die 3-1 deficit in games. The final game was an eight-hitter in which Bob struck out eight to set a World Series record of thirty-five strikeouts in one Series.

The Cardinals have not won another pennant since 1968, but Bob had remained one of the National League's most accomplished pitchers. He was 20-13 in 1969 and 23-7 in 1970, a year in which he won his second Cy Young Award, in which he led the major leagues in victories. In 1971, Bob slumped slightly to a 16-13 record, but had a 3.04 ERA and struck out 185 batters. Five of his victories were shutouts, and he completed twenty of his thirty-one starts.

Now, at the age of thirty-seven, Bob Gibson feels he has two or three more seasons of baseball ahead of him. "I won't think about retiring until I don't think I can win any more, and I haven't reached that stage yet," he says.

Bob Gibson has escaped his ghetto. He is in the rarified atmosphere of a $150,000-per-year salary from the Cardinals, plus the supplemental income he derives from several business endeavors.

He has a television show in Omaha, comments on American Basketball Association games, and has investments, businesses and guaranteed security for the future that few men achieve.

"I am a black man, and I have all this," he says. "I did it because I was able to play baseball. Ten years ago there were restaurants I couldn't eat in and hotels I couldn't sleep in, and if I wasn't Bob Gibson they might still be closed to me. I don't want that kind of artificial equality. I'm praying for the day when the color of a man's skin won't mean a thing.

"I am grateful for the ability I have to play baseball, but I would rather be known as Bob Gibson, a man, than Bob Gibson, a baseball star. I haven't forgotten my childhood, but I'm willing to try."

Bob Gibson is quite a man, and only partly because he is quite a pitcher.

Jim Palmer

Even after firing a no-hitter against the Oakland A's on August 13, 1969, Jim Palmer did not feel secure about his future as a major-league pitcher.

"I'm reserved about success" he said that day. "I've had to come back about four or five times in the last two years because my arm has been hurt just about everywhere. Who knows what is next?"

What followed for Palmer was a welcome rest from physical complications. And along with good health came good pitching. Despite

37

spending 41 days on the disabled list just prior to his no-hit effort, Palmer fashioned a 16-4 record in 1969 and went on to register four straight twenty-victory seasons for the Baltimore Orioles.

Shortly after being voted the American League Cy Young Award winner for 1973, the tall righthander reflected on his early difficulties.

"There have been hundreds of young pitchers who never reached their potential because of arm injuries. I was just one of the lucky ones who found out what the problems were before too much damage was done.

"Since 1969, I've been very fortunate to avoid injuries and you need a little good luck to win 20 four years in a row. I'm really thrilled about winning the Cy Young award," Palmer added. "It's nice to know that you're recognized as the best pitcher in the league. Every year I've been close (in the balloting) but this year I finally made it.

"I actually felt"—the forthright Palmer confessed—"that I was the best pitcher in the American League in 1973. I don't know exactly what the criteria for winning the Cy Young

award is, but I guess in my case, it went to a balanced performance."

In 1973, Palmer led the American League with a 2.40 earned run average and topped the circuit's twelve twenty-game winners with a .709 victory percentage. His strikeout total (158), however, was less than half that of second-place Cy Young Award vote-getter Nolan Ryan, who fanned a record 383.

"Ryan has a super arm and used it to get a tremendous amount of strikeouts and broke records," observed Palmer, "but he went more for strikeouts than putouts. I'd rather allow a batter to hit my first pitch 280 feet into an outfielder's glove than strike him out five or six pitches later. It's easier on the arm."

The Ryan Express was not too surprised at his second place finish. "At first I thought it would be Catfish Hunter," the Angel fireballer noted, "but the more I thought about it, I figured it would be Palmer. He had the more impressive statistics."

California general manager Harry Dalton thought Ryan should have won because he pitched two no-hitters and missed two others by a matter of inches, but he had only praise for Palmer. "I can't really quarrel with the selection of Palmer. He's an excellent choice and I think he was helped by the fact he's been an outstanding pitcher for many years but never before won the award."

Dalton's point may be well taken. Although the Cy Young voting is based on performance in a single season, it would have been difficult for the voters to pass over Palmer's fourth straight twenty-victory season and his 122-57 major-league career record in favor of a strikeout sensation who has won twenty only once and has a losing (69-70) lifetime record in the big leagues.

In pressure games, Palmer often becomes a strikeout pitcher. He has excelled in post-season play. He has struck out 35 batters in 47 2/3 innings of World Series pitching to fashion a 3-1 record and his championship playoff series mark is even better.

In the 1973 playoffs against the World Champion Oakland A's, for instance, Palmer fanned 15 in fifteen innings for a playoff career total of 39 in forty-two innings. He accounted for one of two Oriole victories in the five-game series to run his playoff record to 4-0.

After an ineffective second start, Palmer

came back to contribute four and one-third innings of shutout relief in the finale, but it was too late for the Orioles as Jim Hunter flipped a 3-0 shutout.

Hunter, who finished third in the 1973 Cy Young vote, was asked during the playoffs who should get the award. "Jim Palmer is the best pitcher in the league," the A's righthander said without hesitation. "He deserves it all the way."

One reason why Palmer has become a superstar is his ability to make intelligent adjustments to his own particular strengths and weaknesses on a given day.

Veteran Oriole catcher Andy Etchebarren talks about the many Jim Palmers he has worked with. "Some days," Etchebarren explains, "Jim wins with his curveball and he almost always has a pretty good fastball, which is what most batters are looking for. Even when he doesn't have either one, he's liable to beat you on brains alone."

In the first inning of the first 1973 playoff game against Oakland, Palmer had an overpowering fastball but it was moving so much that it was difficult to control.

Palmer was on the mound for 16 minutes

throwing 29 pitches, walking the first two batters and generally fighting to stay in the game, but he turned it all around, striking out the next three men and coasting for his first playoff shutoff.

"For the first four or five innings," said World Series MVP Reggie Jackson, "Palmer threw as hard, if not harder, than Nolan Ryan. And, after the first few batters, he knew exactly where the ball was going. Man throws like that, he doesn't lose no games."

* * *

James Alvin Palmer was born in New York City on October 15, 1945, but his childhood was divided among New York, Scottsdale, Arizona and Hollywood, California (his step-father, Max Palmer, sometimes worked as a movie extra in Hollywood.) Jim made good use of his athletic abilities to help him adjust from one home town to another.

"You meet new friends quickly if you are involved in athletics," Palmer observes, "and I played every sport I could find time for."

At Scottsdale, he earned All-State high school honors in football, basketball and baseball. Despite numerous college basketball and football scholarship offers, he decided to accept a $60,000 bonus for signing with Baltimore in 1963.

Palmer was able to overcome the customary wildness of a young fastball pitcher very early in his professional career. As an eighteen-year-old, Palmer issued 130 free passes in one hundred and twenty-nine innings during his first professional season at Aberdeen in the Northern League. His three losses in 14 decisions were directly attributable to the walks he permitted and the next spring, Palmer surprised the Orioles with new-found control and was promoted to the major leagues at the tender age of nineteen.

"There were mental as well as physical adjustments to make," the friendly, articulate Palmer recalls. "When you are young, there is a temptation to try and throw the ball past everybody, all the time. You have more confidence in your velocity than you do in your ability to throw the ball to the right spot at the right time."

Palmer, a natural athlete, learned quickly. He walked only 56 batters in ninety-two innings of his rookie season with Baltimore, winning five of nine and striking out 75.

The next season, he was the talk of the American League, winning fifteen games as a twenty-year-old. Then came the 1966 World Series against the Los Angeles Dodgers, and Palmer became the youngest man ever to fashion a series shutout.

"That was a fantastic thrill," Palmer remembers, "and it was a shocker to a lot of people. The Dodgers had Sandy Koufax and Don Drysdale and were figured to beat us on pitching. I don't usually think much about who I'm pitching against but facing a legend like Koufax in the World Series gave me a few chills."

Palmer was so nervous and distracted that he blanked the Dodgers while his team scored six runs to defeat the great lefthander in his last major-league appearance.

"I was just about on top of the world after the Series," Palmer says, "but I didn't stay up there very long." The 6-3, 195-pound righthander began to have arm problems in 1967 and pitched in only nine games for the Orioles.

When he did pitch for Baltimore in 1967, Palmer still managed to get people out, despite a sore shoulder. That was part of his problem, in fact. He didn't *appear* hurt, and there were some who diagnosed his problem as 80 per cent mental.

Palmer felt the pain, however, and knew he was not helping his condition by continuing to pitch. The problem was complicated when another young Baltimore ace, Dave McNally, also was sidelined with arm trouble and, suddenly, the Orioles were desperate for pitching help.

Palmer, an intelligent young man, began to read up on arm, shoulder and elbow injuries, and that didn't particularly endear him to some of the Oriole brass, either. The credibility gap became geographical when Baltimore decided to send him to Rochester.

Palmer, not particularly impressed with the travel cure, observed: "If my arm hurts in Baltimore, it's going to hurt in Rochester." And it did. It also hurt in Miami of the Florida League later that summer.

The pressure on Palmer increased when coach Billy Hunter helped McNally stretch out the tendons in his arm with a gradual, controlled throwing program. McNally became the prize pupil in a winter conditioning class conducted by Hunter. Palmer kept his legs in shape, but felt continual twinges in his arm.

In 1968, McNally battled back for a 22-10 record and the American League Comeback of the Year award, while Palmer toured places like Rochester, Miami and Elmira. He pitched only thirty-seven innings, all in the minor leagues, and didn't win a game.

Not one major-league team wanted him at the $25,000 waiver price in September of 1968, and both Kansas City and Seattle passed him up in the expansion draft that winter. The Orioles sent him to Peurto Rico to pitch winter ball and there Palmer got some help. An anti-inflammation drug made a big difference in the shoulder. So did the discovery that one of Palmer's legs was shorter than the other. The arm and back strain on his right side was lessened by inserting a pad under his left foot.

So equipped, Palmer returned to the Orioles for spring training of 1969. When the season started, he dazzled American League batters with his fastball once again. He had won nine of his first eleven decisions when a separated back muscle put him back on the disabled list for another forty-one days. His arm, however,

48

was not a problem this time and he bounced back quickly with a no-hitter in his second start. He finished with a 16-4 season.

Despite the comeback in 1969 and the 20-10, 20-9, 21-10 and 22-9 seasons that followed directly, there are some who doubt that Palmer ever completely regained his 1966 velocity.

"I can remember facing him when he was a rookie," says former American League Most Valuable Player Carl Yastrzemski, "and being amazed at how well he controlled that super fastball. He had such poise that it was hard to believe he was so young. Then he disappeared and, when he came back to the bigs, he was even smarter but I don't think he's ever been quite so quick as he was the first time around."

Among the "what ifs" baseball fans throw around are questions about how many victories Palmer might have earned if not for his arm troubles and how much more famous he might be if he had played in New York or Los Angeles instead of Baltimore.

A strikingly handsome man with a gracious, easy manner, Palmer might have rivaled Tom Seaver for Madison Avenue's favor, especially since he was born in New York. In Baltimore, where the fans often take the Orioles for granted, Palmer's off-season activities are much less commercial than those of many stars of lesser accomplishment.

An outstanding golfer, Palmer travels to warm-weather areas to compete in celebrity tournaments and other sports events. He once won a sports car for coming closest to the pin in a driving contest. His off-season activities also include volunteer work with charities and playing basketball for the Orioles' team, which he leads in scoring or rebounding almost every winter.

"Jim is one of those people who can do anything that involves timing and coordination," says teammate Marv Rettunmund. "He's a natural . . . on a baseball field, a pool table, a tennis court and especially on a golf course. I really believe he could be a golf pro if he dropped everything else and gave it all his attention.

"He may be the first pitcher to pinch hit for a designated-hitter," the jovial outfielder continued, referring to Palmer's prowess as a batter. "He can do just about anything he puts his mind to. It's a good thing he's such a nice guy or I'd definitely have to hate him."

A game, a sport, a challenge—they all interest Palmer, even if the activity isn't in the big time. He used to test his reflexes with former roommate Dave Leonhard, who would throw two baseballs to Palmer at the same time to see if he could catch one in each hand.

"I once caught both balls twenty times in a row," Palmer says with half a smile and half a look of real accomplishment. "I can catch three at once, too. I'd like to try four but Dave could never get the knack of throwing that many at once."

In explaining how he helped outfielder Don Baylor out of a 1973 slump, Palmer mentioned that he had hit .230 in 1972 "by just looking for the fastball all the time." It is just another indication of how the man makes it all look easy.

Oriole manager Earl Weaver, in fact, believes Palmer's smoothness and easy-going manner contribute to the way the media overlook him.

"People tend to take Palmer for granted," Weaver noted during the 1973 season. "He's not a very controversial person, I guess; no gimmicks, no wild talk. I can remember when people said it was easy to win twenty for this club because we had so many good hitters. Well, now we have to scratch for every run and he's still a twenty-game winner."

Palmer has come a long way from the frustration and uncertainity of 1967 and '68 to become the ace of the Oriole staff. He has been Baltimore's only twenty-game winner for the past two seasons, after teaming with McNally and Mike Cuellar for the previous two seasons.

In 1970 and 1971 the three men won 129 and lost 49 as the Orioles won their second and third straight American League pennants. Palmer however, admitted at times to feeling as though he was regarded as the "other" pitcher—behind McNally and Cuellar.

In 1969, Palmer was the No. 3 man in Weaver's World Series rotation and got into only one chapter of the Amazin' Met's success story. He started the third game and was victimized by Tommie Agee's first-inning homer and two spectacular catches by the same centerfielder in a 5-0 loss. New York's five-game putdown of what was supposed to be the best team in baseball disturbed Palmer and his mates a great deal and they were back in 1970 to make amends.

This time the opposition came from the Cincinnati Reds, and Johnny Bench predicted the crucial game would be the first one against Palmer. "If we can beat their ace in the opener, we'll be on our way."

The Reds not only failed to beat Palmer in game one (he allowed only five hits in 8 2/3 innings of a 4-3 victory) but they failed again in game four. Cincinnati beat relief pitcher Eddie Watt in that one, but the Orioles took game five to become world champions for the second time in Palmer's career.

It was not until 1972 that he was acknowledged by Weaver as the No. 1 pitcher on the staff and, it goes without saying, that you can't be No. 1 in the league unless you are first tagged No. 1 on your team.

After Palmer had stopped his seventh Oriole losing streak of three games or more, Weaver said, "Jim has become our stopper. We keep getting in trouble and he keeps bailing us out. He is the guy who is winning the big games for us."

The final step toward a Cy Young Award came when Palmer registered a fourth straight superior season.

As usual, however, there were some who took him for granted. In the wake of spectacular no-hit successes by National League transplants Jim Bibby and Nolan Ryan, there were people who claimed that a pitcher's life was considerably easier in the American League.

"A guy with a good fastball has it made over there," said Met third-baseman Wayne Garrett one day. "Look at Jim Palmer with the Orioles. He wins twenty games every year without even trying. He probably couldn't do that in the National League because there are a lot more good fastball hitters."

Asked about Garrett's claim, ex-Oriole Frank Robinson, who has earned Most Valuable Player honors in both leagues, had a different theory. "No, I'd disagree with Garrett on that," he said.

"I'd say Jim Palmer has enough stuff to win twenty in the American, National, Japanese, Mexican or any other league I've ever seen."

Vida Blue

Vida Blue has been there and back at the age of 24, and he gives the distinct impression that he didn't enjoy the trip.

The ups have been incredibly steep in Blue's short career, and the downs have been sudden and jarring. From an amazing 24-8 record in 1971, Blue fell to 6-10 after a bitter 1972 salary squabble with Oakland owner Charlie Finley. The fireballing lefthander bounced back in 1973 with a 20-9 record, but made no secret of his unhappiness with the A's.

"Pitching is just a job," Blue said often

during the 1973 season. He was critical of the way manager Dick Williams employed him and he refused to talk about Finley, except to say, "He pays the salaries, I believe."

Although Blue won twenty games in 1973, he struggled through the first three-fourths of the season and never regained the overwhelming dominance he enjoyed during the first half of 1971.

"It may be mental," said Reggie Jackson early in the 1973 season. "You don't know what it's like to play major-league baseball. No one knows unless he plays it. The pressures, the troubles. Any little things can affect a player."

"I don't know if Vida will do what he did two years ago, if he will again pitch the way he did. But, if he doesn't by the middle of next season, I'll say this. The only thing that will help him is a trade."

An unhappy Blue won twenty games for Oakland in '73, and so there is every reason to suspect that a reasonably content Blue could win more. The pitcher insists he is doing all he can.

"I'm me, just trying to win," he explains. "I'll do anything I can to win. Even if it means

pitching righthanded." The lefthander's use of sarcasm has increased considerably since he was a friendly, enthusiastic rookie in 1971.

"For every game I've thrown out on the mound," Blue said before his late-season surge in 1973, "I've thrown ten in the bullpen. And eight of those have been perfect games.

"It's get on the mound, four innings, see ya later," added Blue in criticism of Williams' tendency to replace his starters quickly. "It's five innings and see ya later. A complete game? It means the law of averages just caught up with you."

Blue's late start after his long holdout in 1972 apparently led to his difficulties. Blue wanted approximately $90,000, and Finley simply refused to negotiate from that figure.

By the time Blue signed, for $63,000, including some bonus money, it was early May. As is often the case, the youngster tried to rush his return and lost a lot of the zip on his fastball. He was moody, resentful and angry at almost everyone, including the press and the public.

The 1973 edition of Vida Rochelle Blue, Jr., was not much happier, but he was considerably more successful. Most observers claim he never regained all the velocity on his fast-ball, but A's catcher Ray Fosse says he came very close.

"Vida got faster as the season went along. And he's come up with some sort of hard-breaking ball that Wes Stock (pitching coach) and I have been trying to get him to throw more often. It's a cross between a slider and a curve; Vida calls it a slurve. The pitch is really going to help him because nobody can just stand up there and keep looking for the smoke anymore.

"Blue's fastball just explodes," Fosse explains. "The main thing about catching him is to try and keep his pitches down as much as possible. When he throws the hard one low in the strike zone, I don't think there's anybody who can hit him.

"A lot of times," Fosse adds, "I've missed fastballs over my head, over the hitter's head. It's just that the ball explodes. Then they come around and ask me whether my shoulder is bothering me or my arm is hurting but it's just that when he throws the ball high, it just takes off. It really rises in a hurry."

Comparing Blue's approach to the game with that of the other A's twenty-game winners, Ken Holtzman and Jim Hunter, Fosse notes that Vida occasionally toys with a hitter. "Where Kenny and Catfish want to get the game over as quickly as possible, Vida has a little bounce to him. He wants to have a little fun out there.

"Maybe he just wants to stand out there on the mound and have the hitter say, 'Hey, let's throw the ball,' and then he throws it right by him. I'm telling you, that can happen."

It happened often in 1971. Blue stormed on the scene and won ten in a row with complete game victories, allowing six or fewer hits in each one. The rookie seemed to have fun off the mound, too. He appeared relaxed, articulate, cooperative and buoyant. He smiled often and handled the pressure so easily that some people thought he thrived on it.

But some time late in the season, after Blue had begun to lose almost as often as he won, the constant glare of the spotlight began to make him uncomfortable. He became defensive, reacted sarcastically when questions from the media became repetitious and made it very evident that he was no longer enjoying his sudden fame. Blue was tired and edgy, and that was not surprising.

Blue's disenchantment with the trappings of success might never have disintegrated into bitterness if not for his well-publicized battle with Finley ... but the battle did happen. Blue felt he had given a lot. He had done his part and more. He was sure he was worth $90,000 after becoming a folk hero all over the nation in just one year.

He was the youngest pitcher ever to win the Cy Young Award as the American League's best pitcher. He was the country's No. 1 sports hero. How could Finley turn him down? When the A's owner did just that, Blue thought there would be such an outcry against him that he would have to pay up. But that's not what happened. It was the young superstar who had to relent, settling for $25,000 less than he had hoped for and reporting late to training camp as a beaten holdout instead of a conquering hero.

But Blue's later troubles do not erase memories of the way he was for most of the 1971 season. The young lefty dealt with the demands on his free time graciously and he seemed to take the adulation and constant attention in stride.

There were endless requests for interviews,

appearances, photography sessions, banquet speeches and television shows. If Blue made a mistake, it was that he didn't want to turn anybody down.

The veteran stars usually understand the pressures and learn along the way to the top how to budget their time to meet the increased demands. They also learn to gauge their own strength and develop priorities in order to prevent outside activities from hurting their athletic careers. Those who rise gradually to prominence can observe others and benefit from their experience, but Blue had to find out for himself. That can be difficult.

Seldom has one player propelled his team so far, and never has a player so young accomplished so much in his first full season as a major leaguer. No one can take that away from Vida Blue, and there is no limit to what he can accomplish in the future.

Vida Blue opened the 1971 season as an almost unknown factor. The pitching staff of the Athletics was already very powerful. The presence of such hurlers as John "Blue Moon" Odom, Jim "Catfish" Hunter, Chuck Dobson, Diego Segui and Rollie Fingers seemed to dictate against the likelihood of a young pitcher making his way into the regular rotation, for not only were Oakland's pitchers sound and effective, they were blessed with youth, stamina, enthusiasm and great potential.

Blue was the youngest pitcher on the staff, just twenty-one when the team gathered for spring training in Mesa, Arizona. He had shown some outstanding potential the season before, when he had been called up to finish the major-league season with the Athletics after spending much of the summer pitching for Iowa of the American Association.

He had appeared in six games for Oakland in 1970, winning two games and escaping defeat, striking out thirty-five men in thirty-nine innings. But it was the way in which he swept past American League hitters that intrigued the Athletics.

In his second big-league start, September 11, he spun a one-hitter against the Kansas City Royals, and he followed that up ten days later with a no-hitter against the pennant-bound Minnesota Twins, his attempt at a perfect game spoiled when he walked home-run slugger Harmon Killebrew in the fourth inning.

His pitch was a fastball, one he threw ninety

percent of the time that day. It was not just another good fastball, but a special one. It was a fastball impressive enough to be compared with those of Sam McDowell of the Cleveland Indians, Nolan Ryan of the New York Mets, Bob Veale of the Pittsburgh Pirates, Don Gullett of the Cincinnati Reds.

In short, it was an extraordinary fastball, the kind that blurred as it crossed home plate, the sort that looked impossible to hit, and often was.

So the Athletics, feeling they had a special young man on their staff, gave Vida Blue every chance to earn a spot in the 1971 rotation.

He did not let them down. His spring training was a wonderland of fastballs and strikeouts, scoreless innings and laughter, bats stinging the hands of those hitters who made contact. The manager of the team, Dick Williams, was in his second year with Oakland. He had been named to the position in 1970, having left the Boston Red Sox, and he brought with him eighteen years of experience as a player, two years as an International League manager and three years with the Red Sox, one of which brought Boston a pennant, its first since 1946.

"I knew we had something special in Vida," he says. "The kid just threw smoke. I have seen few pitchers throw any harder, and I'm not at all sure they were any faster. Maybe just as fast, but not faster, and I'm talking about all the great ones, like Bob Feller and Sandy Koufax and Jim Maloney and Herb Score. But Vida was so young, and so inexperienced."

Yet the manager's natural reluctance to place so great a responsibility in the hands of one so young soon melted in the heat of the Arizona sunshine, for Vida Blue seemed older than his years, mature beyond his limited experience.

"After a while," Williams says, "I'd find myself thinking of him as a veteran, and then all of a sudden I'd remember he was just a kid. It was quite an experience. I never had one like it before, and I'm glad I did because I don't think it will happen for me again. He's a pleasure to manage. He's the nicest kid in the world."

So, despite the odds and the past teachings of so many veterans, Williams decided not only to make room for Vida Blue on the Athletics' staff, but to give him the honor of starting the season. It was against the Washington Senators (now the Texas Rangers) in the so-called "Presidential opener" in Washington. This game took place annually, one day before any other teams played their first game.

Was it a triumph? Did it result in a superlative effort? Did the honor fit the man? No. Blue lost to the weak-hitting Senators, and the fact that he lost the game, 8-0, was noted in the newspapers only because it was the only game of the day. It appeared that he was destined to sink into the temporary anonymity of so many other young pitchers who arrive with speed and potential and then settle down to mediocrity until they learn to pitch as well as throw. Even Sandy Koufax went that route.

But not Vida Blue. He had something to do and the next time out he started doing it.

Indeed, from that opening-day loss until the traditional mid-season break for the All-Star Game, Vida Blue won seventeen of his next nineteen decisions, captivating the nation's fans with his 17-3 record.

As his winning streak grew, so did his horde of fans, and teams around the league viewed his arrival with mixed emotions. They were afraid to face him, but they were pleased with his appearance in their stadiums, for soon his presence meant the sale of as many as 10,000 additional tickets.

In fact, he helped the Athletics become a financial success at home. The Oakland fans had become accustomed to dull, uninspired baseball from their relatively new team, and they made it a common practice to stay away from all the games, unless a contending team or a superstar was coming to town.

The Athletics finished Vida Blue's first full season with a total attendance of 914,993, hardly impressive when compared with the figures drawn by such powerful franchises as the New York Mets, the Los Angeles Dodgers, the San Francisco Giants and the Philadelphia Phillies. But just a year before, Oakland had drawn a total of just 778,355, despite the fact that they had battled the Minnesota Twins down to the final weeks of the schedule before finishing second in the American League's Western Division.

The only two games during the month of September when the Athletics drew more than 10,000 fans at home were when Blue was the starting pitcher. One of them was Vida Blue Night, during which team owner Charles Finley tore up Vida's contract, presented him with a $5,000 raise on the spot, and also made him a gift of a new, blue (what else?) Cadillac, with California license plates that read, simply, V-BLUE.

When Vida was at the peak of his winning streak in June, the average home attendance in Oakland was 21,314, the highest figure by far for any month in the history of the franchise.

On the road, Vida was as much, perhaps more, of an attraction. He appeared as the starting pitcher in New York twice, and each time the Yankees drew inordinately large crowds. The second time, in fact, old Yankee Stadium was crammed with more than 40,000 customers. The Yankees sold special scorecards that night, with an insert printed on blue paper to mark Vida's appearance. He did not let the fans down, either, winning the game, 6-4.

Afterwards, a throng of newsmen and radio-television interviewers descended on him in the cramped quarters of the visitors' dressing room. Blue exhibited his unusual good humor and stoic patience.

He had to stand on a stool to make himself

heard and seen, and the highlight of the interview was his response to a question about his own opinion of his talent.

"Would you compare yourself to Sandy Koufax?" someone wondered.

"How can I do that?" Vida responded, laughing. "I'm black, and he's Jewish."

Vida tailed off to a 7-5 record for the second half of the 1971 season, and finished with a 24-8 record, disappointing those who said he was a sure-shot thirty-game winner. The pressure had finally affected him, and he was the first to admit he was tired; more tired than any young athlete should be in a normal season.

But his glowing statistics showed what he had accomplished.

His 24-8 log was spiced with 301 strikeouts ... with 312 innings pitched ... with eight shutouts ... with a one-hitter, a two-hitter, a pair of three-hitters and a half-dozen four-hitters ... with twenty-four complete games in thirty-nine starts.

His 1.82 earned run average led the league, and was second in the majors to the 1.76 registered by Tom Seaver of the New York Mets.

Adding wonder to his performance was the

fact that prior to the 1971 season the most games he had ever won was twelve, in the minor leagues; the most strikeouts he had ever recorded was 231, in his first year of minor-league ball; the most innings he had ever worked was 152, also in his first minor-league season.

It was small wonder, then, that the Baseball Writers Association of America bestowed on Vida Blue its highest honor by naming him the 1971 Cy Young Award winner. He was the youngest recipient in the eighteen-year history of the award, the previous youngest being Dean Chance, who was twenty-three when he won it in 1964 as the star of the Minnesota Twins' staff.

Some detractors—and there are always detractors—claimed that Vida was handed the award solely for his performance during the first half of the season, that over the entire season Detroit's Mickey Lolich had been the more consistent, and therefore the more deserving.

There was no doubt, however, as to Vida's popularity or his impact on the American League, for the announcement of his Cy Young victory was quickly followed by the surprising

news that he had been named the league's
Most Valuable Player as well.

What a season it had been.

The six-foot, 190-pound lefthander had been
a shot in the arm to the sagging fortunes not
only of the Athletics but of the American
League, which had begun to suffer from the
monotonous winning habits of the powerful
Baltimore Orioles and the consequent lack of
exciting pennant races.

Blue added drama and color to the game,
and the season was an artistic success for him
beyond his wildest dreams.

National magazines used his picture on their
covers and devoted full pages to his exploits.
They reached back to his ghetto childhood in
Mansfield, Louisiana. They interviewed towns-
people back home. They interviewed his mother
and his friends. They fought for every bit of
information, every exclusive photograph.

There was a picture of Vida leaping high
into the air and clicking his heels while run-
ning in the outfield, and the national wire
services released it to thousands of newspapers
throughout the country.

There was speculation on Blue's other athletic abilities . . . on his love of football . . . on

his bachelorhood. Wherever he went, reporters and photographers trailed in his wake.

"I just can't believe all this is happening to me," he said. "Why, last year nobody knew who I was, and now I have to hide to eat dinner or go see a movie."

It was a case of a young man being caught up in the publicity-whirl that only the United States can set in motion, and Vida loved it.

* * *

Vida Blue was born on July 28, 1949, in Mansfield, La. He was a three-sport participant in high school and then entered Southern University in Baton Rouge, La., on a football scholarship.

But, by the time he was eighteen, he had signed a contract with the Athletics. Part of the reason he spurned the football scholarship and the opportunity to attend college was his determination to be a financial aid to his widowed mother and his five brothers and sisters. The Athletics had offered a $35,000 bonus, and it was too much for a poor kid to walk away from. When he received the money, he bought an eight-room house for his family and helped send two of his sisters to Grambling College.

At eighteen Vida was on the staff of the Burlington farm team in the Midwest League. Although his record was 8-11, he led the league with his 231 strikeouts in 104 innings. His fastball was a live and wicked weapon, and the Athletics decided to see what he could do throwing it against major-league batters.

So in August of 1969 they summoned young Blue to the major leagues, where he appeared in a dozen games, worked forty-two innings, compiled a 1-1 mark and struck out twenty-four batters. It was enough of a showing for the team to tremble with anticipation, for here was a teenager who could beat major leaguers. Here, indeed, was a very special young man.

"One more year in the minors," said Charles Finley, "and Vida Blue will be ready for the big time for keeps." His analysis was echoed by manager Williams, who had just become the Athletics' field leader that season and who couldn't wait until Blue became a member of his staff.

Thus it was that 1970 dawned with Vida Blue on the Iowa team of the American Association, and despite several leaves to satisfy

Vida Blue

his Armed Services obligations, he built a 12-3
record for Iowa with a league-leading 165
strikeouts in just 133 innings. His earned run
average (2.17) and low number of walks
(fifty-five) offered further proof that he had
become a dominant pitcher.

Finding it unnecessary for Vida to acquire
any further minor-league seasoning, the Athletics decided to bring him up when the American Association schedule ran its course. He
joined the Oakland team in September and
appeared in six games, long enough to gain his
one-hitter against Kansas City and his classic
no-hitter against Minnesota.

Quickly stories of this incredibly hard-
throwing rookie spread throughout both
leagues, and several teams attempted to con-
vince the Athletics to trade him. "We turned
down some fine deals," Finley says, but will
not identify the teams that sought Blue or the
players offered in exchange. "Let's just say
they were attractive offers, and more than
anything else that made us determined to keep
him.

"We had the hitting and the defense, and
what we needed was the one super pitcher for

our staff. With Vida, we felt we could have that, too."

But youngsters with less than one season in the major leagues do not command lucrative contracts. Blue himself had no idea of what he was going to be able to accomplish, and so he settled for a rather modest $15,000 salary, with no bonus clauses written in. Bonus clauses, while approved in professional football and basketball, are mysteriously forbidden by major-league baseball.

For their $15,000, the Athletics received a performance worth ten times that much.

After the opening-day loss to Washington, an 8-0 decision in which Vida surrendered four runs but only one earned run, he embarked on a storyland ten-game winning streak, a skein that did not end until May 28 when he lost a 4-3 decision to the Boston Red Sox.

That made his record 10-2, and he increased it to 17-3 by winning four more in succession, then losing another, then winning three more.

Naturally, he was chosen for the American Leagues' All-Star staff; and naturally, he drew the starting assignment from Baltimore's Earl Weaver, who managed the All-Star team.

"What else could I have done?" asked Weaver. "If I didn't start the kid, half the country would have sent me nasty letters."

The Athletics, meanwhile, had spread-eagled the rest of the American League West, and cake-walked to their divisional championship. Blue did not do as well in the second half of the season, but what he had accomplished in the first half, plus the contributions of such as Hunter (21-11), Segui (10-8) and Odom (10-12) made the team impossible to catch for the remainder of the season.

They won their division by a wide margin, and prepared to face the World Champion Baltimore Orioles in the American League's best-of-five playoff series, with the winner advancing to the World Series.

The first game, according to both managers, was to be the pivotal one. Each team was leading with its best pitcher—Blue for Oakland, Dave McNally for Baltimore—and in a short series the first game is the all-important one. Added to that is the psychological edge of knowing you have beaten the other team's strongest pitcher, which is no small mental advantage.

Thus Blue, with his 24-8 record, faced the

21-5 McNally on October 3, in Baltimore's Memorial Stadium.

The game proved to be somewhat of a letdown, since neither pitcher was able to last more than seven innings. Blue, who had twice beaten Baltimore during the season, was staked to a three-run lead and going into the fourth inning had yet to surrender a hit.

Oakland had scored twice in the second, when third baseman Sal Bando led off with a double and scored on a triple by Angel Mangual, who came home moments later when catcher Dave Duncan doubled. McNally was in trouble, but he received a break when, with Blue at bat, Duncan broke for home on an apparent squeeze play. But Vida did not offer at the pitch, and Duncan was tagged out in a rundown.

The third Oakland run came in the fourth, when outfielder Tommy Davis lined a single and rode home on Mangual's double.

But Blue could not hold his advantage. In the fourth he gave up the first Baltimore hit to second baseman Dave Johnson, a double. Then outfielder Marv Rettunmund drove him in with another double.

The end for Vida came in the seventh. After

outfielder Frank Robinson opened the inning with a walk, third baseman Brooks Robinson singled. Frank took third on a fly to right by catcher Andy Etchebarren and scored when shortshop Mark Belanger singled to center.

Pinch hitter Curt Motton doubled home Brooks, and outfielder Paul Blair doubled in Belanger and Motton. Rollie Fingers relieved Blue in the eighth, and the Athletics, their ace having been driven from the mound, went down listlessly in the next two games, 5-1 and 5-3.

The splendid season was over for Vida Blue.

But what fascinates his teammates and fans and worries his opponents is the future Vida apparently has as a superstar.

"If he was able to do that much in his first full year," says teammate Curt Blefary, a power-hitting first-baseman, "what will he be like five years from now, when he improves his curve and gets smarter? If he gets very much better, they'll have to pass a law making him pitch underhanded or something."

Hall of Famer Bob Feller, whose fastball was said to be the best in the history of base-ball, was in Cleveland late in the season and saw Blue beat the hometown Indians. Afterwards, he sat down to dinner with a writer and offered his opinion of the young star.

"He throws faster than most people I've seen," Feller said. "What makes him really tough is the velocity of his fastball. It seems to pick up speed as it reaches home plate, and when he takes a little bit off it, he throws the hitters' rhythm way out. Once he develops a good curve and a changeup, I think he'll be a consistent twenty-game winner. He could be the best."

The temptation for the writer was too juicy to pass up.

"Who was faster, Bob, you or Koufax?"

"I was," said Bob Feller.

"And who is faster, you or Vida Blue?"

Feller started to answer, then paused, finally grinned. "He can be," said the Hall of Fame pitcher. "I really think he can throw the ball faster than I did."

No finer tribute is possible. It is as good as Babe Ruth wishing Hank Aaron well in his quest for the Bambino's all-time home-run record.

Blue never completely regained the Feller-type fastball after his pre-season battle with Finley in 1972, and he finished an unhappy

6-10 regular season as a relief pitcher. He grumbled about being assigned to the bullpen but carried the A's into the World Series with four shutout innings in the fifth playoff game against Detroit.

In the World Series, Blue was not quite so spectacular, losing one game and permitting four earned runs in eight and two-thirds innings of relief work. Not even when the A's beat the Cincinnati Reds for the world championship did the young lefthander let down his guard and enjoy the occasion.

In 1973 Blue regained his role as a starter, but manager Williams drew his ire for replacing him quickly. Vida had won only nine of sixteen decisions by mid-season but then he began to throw more breaking balls and his fastball began to pop into the catcher's glove. His first 10-plus strikeout game didn't come until September 10, but he finished very strong for a 20-9 record.

Indeed, if you add Blue's 1973 late-season 12-2 record to his 17-3 mark for the first half of 1971, the totals are an amazing 29-5. Many people believe Vida is capable of that kind of season.

Blue did not continue to sparkle in the 1973

playoffs and World Series, however. He lost one game against Baltimore, and another against the New York Mets.

Although he didn't take part in the shouting, Blue was the center of one of the smaller controversies of the turbulent Series.

Blue had squandered a 4-0 lead in the seventh inning of game No. 4 when Andy Etchebarren capped a Baltimore surge with a three-run homer.

"We had them by the nostrils and we let them get away from us," relief ace Rollie Fingers muttered, after Fingers had given up an eighth-inning homer to Bobby Grich that produced a 5-4 Oriole triumph.

Blue Moon Odom thought the remark was critical of Blue and jumped to his defense. Ironically, it was an angry confrontation between Odom and Blue the previous year in Detroit that had punctuated the World Series.

"You shouldn't be talking," Odom said to Fingers. "If you don't give up that homer, we don't lose the game." That disturbance was soon forgotten in the continuing furor over Finley attempting to "fire" Mike Andrews after the secondbaseman made two errors in the second game.

Vida Blue

Reggie Jackson just laughed when someone asked if the A's problems upset their ability to perform on the field. Where once Jackson had stressed the difficulty of playing when things went wrong, the star outfielder indicated he and his team-mates had become so accustomed to controversy that it didn't matter anymore.

"Controversies don't bother us because ours start way up there," he said, pointing heavenward toward Finley's executive offices. "We've got controversial management, controversial players and everything else."

It is in such a tumultuous atmosphere that Blue continues his search for greatness.

Nolan Ryan

Veteran catcher Jeff Torborg has been on the receiving end of no-hitters by both Sandy Koufax and Nolan Ryan. He answers the inevitable question with diplomacy and common sense.

"When people want to know if Ryan can throw harder than Koufax could," Torborg explains, "I tell them the truth—you can't really measure any kind of difference at that level. I think you get to a point where a human can't throw a baseball any faster. And they are both at that point."

The soft-spoken country boy from Alvin, Texas, became the pitching sensation of 1973 with two no-hitters and two near misses. Then he broke Koufax' major-league record for strikeouts in one season by fanning Minnesota's Rich Reese with his final pitch of 1973. The comparisons have become unavoidable.

The inside fastball which Reese missed for strike three gave the twenty-six-year-old engineer of "Ryan's Express" 383 strikeouts, one more than Koufax had registered at the height of his career in 1965. At the age of twenty-six, the Dodger lefthander had sixty-eight victories. Ryan has sixty-nine.

It was the fireballing Koufax who established a major-league record by striking out ten or more batters twenty-one times in a single season, and it was Ryan who improved on that by two in 1972.

It was Koufax who set the modern mark (since 1900) for most strikeouts in consecutive seasons (699), and it was Ryan who erased it with 712 in 1972 and '73 with the California Angels.

Ryan appears embarrassed by comparisons with Koufax. He recalls the great lefty with obvious admiration.

"I don't think I will ever see a pitcher as good as Koufax," Ryan says sincerely. "When I was in high school I went from home (Alvin) to Houston to watch him pitch. His fastball did things I never thought a ball could be made to do."

Ryan's fastball does not jump two feet in mid-flight as the Koufax model often did, but it sails and dips, especially when thrown just below thigh level. Ryan, like the young Koufax before him, has difficulty controlling baseballs traveling over 100 miles per hour, but he has harnessed his spectacular ability well enough to become a twenty-game winner.

In 1973, Ryan won his last seven decisions with complete games for a 21-16 record. His record gains added luster from the fact that the Angels team ranked last in the American League in hitting, runs batted in and home runs.

Two no-hitters, twenty-one victories and numerous strikeout records were not enough to earn him the American League's Cy Young Award, however. "I don't know what a guy has to do to win the award," Angel General Manager Harry Dalton said when Jim Palmer's victory over Ryan was announced.

Although Palmer's point total was twenty-six points more than Ryan's, the difference could also be tabulated as a few inches. The inches in question were those that kept Ryan from four no-hitters in 1973, instead of two. Ryan came that close to matching Koufax' career no-hit total in one season. If he had succeeded, the Baseball Writers Association wouldn't even have had to hold its election.

Ryan fired his first no-hitter at Kansas City on May 15. Four days later, at Anaheim, he had another no-hitter going into the eighth. Mark Belanger then looped a short fly to center field that Ken Berry, who was playing unusually deep for the situation, missed by one stride.

The Express not only lost his bid to match Johnny Vander Meer's feat of consecutive no-hitters but wound up losing an eleventh-inning three-hitter to the Baltimore Orioles.

A near miss against the New York Yankees on August 29 was even more a matter of poor support from his fielders. The only "hit" Ryan permitted was a first-inning pop fly off the bat of Thurman Munson which should have been caught easily. Both second-baseman Sandy

Alomar and shortstop Rudi Meoli were in position to catch the ball, and both called for it . . . then both backed off at the same time, allowing it to fall to the turf untouched.

Despite the frustrating circumstances of his two near-misses, Ryan threw no tantrums, just more fastballs. He did not even offer a mild criticism of his teammates' fielding or dwell on what might have been. The Express knows that four no-hitters would have brought a Cy Young Award and maybe even the American League's Most Valuable Player designation, but he didn't let any disappointment show through.

* * *

Lynn Nolan Ryan was born on January 31, 1947, in Refugio, Texas, and grew up in nearby Alvin amidst a quiet country atmosphere he still cherishes. The happiness and contentment of Ryan's early years is reflected by the fact that he still lives in Alvin during the off-season.

An older brother first channeled Ryan's interest to baseball. He would throw to Nolan, six years younger, in the back yard and soon decided that he was dealing with a special talent. The Angel ace remembers, "I started playing catch with him when I was very, very young. As a result, I started playing in the Little League a year or two before a lot of the kids, when I was eight years old.

"Five years later," Ryan recalls with a chuckle, "I was a real veteran when I finished my Little League career. My brother pinned me down one time and asked me where I wanted to play because I was playing a lot of positions without really thinking about it. I told him I wanted to pitch because a pitcher gets more involved in a game than anyone else.

"From that day on," Ryan stresses, "he did everything possible to keep me pitching. He warned me not to fool around with sidearm and three-quarter pitches because I might hurt my arm, so I threw straight overhead and I've never really had serious arm problems. He taught me a lot; it was interest and encouragement."

Ryan fired a no-hitter in a state playoff game for Alvin High School and was chosen to the all-Texas team in 1965, but he wasn't selected by the majors until the Mets took him 295th in the draft that year.

Ryan has found it difficult to adjust to the New York way of life, and returns to Alvin during the off-season with pleasure. He and his beautiful wife, Ruth, own an 8½-acre ranch there and attended classes at Alvin Junior College following Nolan's sensational 1973 season.

The Ryans class choices were practical; income tax preparation and beef cattle raising. Since Ryan reportedly has become the first $100,000 pitcher in Angel history, he is probably paying extra attention to his tax homework.

The Ryans were in the classroom when the Cy Young award results were announced. Earlier in the day, the pitcher's priorities had become apparent. His wife revealed he was "working in the back pasture with the dogs" instead of waiting by the radio.

Although Ryan speaks with an engaging shyness, his words are often quite revealing. He is a private person in some ways, but he is willing to share his baseball life with the public. He talks freely with reporters, signs autographs patiently for the fans and seems to get along well with everyone . . . even with management.

When asked if he would receive a bonus for breaking records or pitching no-hitters, Ryan must have made General Manager Dalton deliriously happy when he replied: "I don't think I deserve it. When I pitch badly, I don't give him any of my salary back."

Ryan works harder on his conditioning than a lot of pitchers and throws more between starts, but the only really unusual feature of his preparation is the series of yoga and stretching exercises he employs.

While standing on his head, with his feet braced up against the left-field wall at Anaheim Stadium, Ryan explained that he practiced yoga physically but did not carry through with the mental gymnastics sometimes associated with it.

"I don't believe in premonitions," he said while upside down. "I really had no premonition I was going to throw a no-hitter in Detroit or anything like that. The only premonition I ever had was when I was in the Little League. We were beaten in a bi-district tournament and we were lined-up on the field for the award ceremonies.

"We were feeling pretty low," Ryan remembered. "Some former major leaguer—I can't remember his name—was passing out the awards. He said, 'One of you boys is going to

be a major leaguer some day.' I thought at the
time I would be that boy."

Ryan's development into a major-league
winner was retarded by the very fact he threw
so hard. He could overpower batters without
a good curveball, without changes of speeds,
without spotting the ball, and without thinking very much about what he was doing.

In his first year of professional baseball,
Ryan won only three of nine decisions for
Marion of the Appalachian League but struck
out 115 batters in seventy-eight innings. The
next season, he led the Western Carolina
League in wins (17), strikeouts (272, in one
hundred and eighty-three innings) and walks
(127) and was second in shutouts (5).

Ryan's impressive effort for Greenville
(17-2) earned him a promotion to Williams-
port late in 1966, and he set an Eastern
League record by striking out 21 Pawtucket
batters in ten innings. He lost, 2-1, on a pair
of unearned runs, but the Mets brought him
up at the end of their season.

Ryan struck out six in three innings on the
mound with New York but he continued to
have control problems. At times, the only way
he could get the ball over the plate was to "take

something off"—reduce the speed—of his fastball. Major-league batters jumped all over
such deliveries.

After 1967 slipped by without much progress—due to an Army Reserve stint and some
minor arm problems—Ryan advanced to the
Mets in 1968. His wildness, his repeated ab-
sences for weekend Reserve duty and a tendency to develop blisters all conspired to keep
Ryan from becoming a winner in New York.

The 6-2, 195-pound righthander finished
only 13 of 73 starts as a Met, winning twenty-
nine and losing thirty-seven as manager Gil
Hodges grew increasingly impatient for
Ryan's potential to pay off in victories.

Ryan often flashed brilliance for one or two
innings in New York, but his first really outstanding effort there came in the playoffs and
World Series of 1969.

In a playoff game against Atlanta, Ryan
struck out seven Braves in seven innings and
allowed only three hits in relief of Gary
Gentry.

In the wild, wild World Series that made
world champions out of Amazin' Mets, Ryan
struck out three Baltimore Orioles in two and
one-third innings to preserve a 5-0 triumph for

Gentry. His control problems, however, seemed to make him unsuitable for a career as a relief pitcher, and so the Mets put him in their regular rotation in 1970.

Ryan pitched some fantastic games but he was inconsistent. His control was never sharp and when he would return after a weekend or a two-week summer camp of Reserve duty, it would take another two weeks for him to find his rhythm . . . and the strike zone.

Met pitching coach Rube Walker, who liked to observe that Ryan's fastball "had a heap of hurry on it," continued to predict great things even after 7-11 and 10-14 seasons.

When trade rumors began circulating near the end of the 1971 season, Walker denied them vehemently. "Nolie has too much potential to trade him," the former Dodger catcher said. "Look at Sandy Koufax and how long it took him to develop. No, they'll never trade this kid."

On December 10, 1971, New York general manager Bob Scheffing did, indeed, trade not only Ryan but outfielder Lee Stanton, pitcher Don Rose and catcher Francisco Estrada to California for the Angels' one-time All-Star shortstop, Jim Fregosi. The fact that Fregosi never was able to make a contribution to the Mets and was subsequently sent back to the American League has served to underscore the Mets' poor judgment. Stanton, in fact, out-hit Fregosi. The deal ranks ahead of even the 1969 Amos Otis-for-Joey Foy fiasco on New York's scale of futility.

There is evidence, however, to suggest that Angel general manager Dalton was more fortunate than wise in acquiring Ryan. He really wanted Gentry. First, he has reported that he had received excellent scouting reports on Gentry during his stay in Baltimore and, secondly, one of the first people he hired in California was Bobby Winkles, who had coached Gentry at Arizona State. When the Mets refused to part with Gentry, Dalton asked for Ryan as second choice. New Yorkers have been sorry ever since.

"I liked playing with the Mets," Ryan says in retrospect, "but they always seemed to be in a pennant race and I never got to work as much as I needed to, just to learn to pitch."

With new surroundings and a chance to pitch (and learn) regularly, Ryan was an instant success with the Angels in 1972. For the first time in six years, he had no Reserve duty to interrupt his progress. Frustrated American League batters were soon marching away from the plate empty-handed in record numbers.

The Express, a nickname both he and his fastball gained from the movie "Von Ryan's Express," set fourteen club records during his first season, led the major leagues in strike-outs (329), and tied for the lead in shutouts (9). He struck out seventeen batters against Minnesota on September 30 to tie an American League record for a nine-inning night game and fanned sixteen on two other occasions.

"I really don't try to strike people out," Ryan often tells disbelieving fastball watchers. "I am not going after strikeout records. My goal is to win twenty games, and if the records come, they come."

Ryan missed the coveted twenty-victory plateau by just one in 1972, but that was pri-marily because opposing pitchers blanked the weak-hitting Californians in six of his fifteen defeats. In absorbing the six losses, the Ex-press yielded ten runs—only six of them earned—for an earned run average of 1.17. In most of his nineteen victories, he left the opposition little choice but to lose. In one particularly forceful effort against Boston, Ryan struck out the side on nine pitches, setting an AL record with eight consecutive strikeouts.

"Ryan would have won 26 or 27 if we could have gotten him three runs a game," said former Angel manager Del Rice, who was replaced by Winkles after the '72 campaign.

Ryan finally reached the twenty victory level in 1973 and it was his most satisfying accomplishment in a season highlighted by two no-hitters and the record 383 strikeouts. "Twenty victories is something you know has to help your team," Ryan notes. "It's also one sign of consistency . . . although that's something I haven't got yet."

The Express admits that breaking the Koufax strikeout record on his final pitch of the season was "cutting it a little too close," but a rainout in Kansas City the final month of the season deprived him of four strikeouts and precious time.

"I would have felt bad if I had come close and didn't make it because of a rainout." Ryan says. "I didn't let it worry me all that much, though. That's life. It's also life when you lose a no-hitter in the first inning on a pop fly that drops between infielders."

The two no-hitters Ryan didn't miss were May 15 (3-0, against Kansas City) and July 15 (6-0, against Detroit). After watching Ryan fan seventeen—the most ever in a no-hitter—Tiger outfielder Dick Sharon exclaimed:

"It's a challenge just to see if you can hit a foul ball off this guy."

Hal McRae moaned a similar observation after Ryan had handcuffed the Royals. "If they had a higher league than the majors, he could be in it. In fact he could *be* it."

Ryan's mother, who has watched her son baffle batters for almost twenty years, was not quite so impressed with the no-hitters. "I think it's wonderful," Mrs. Martha Lee Ryan announced, "but the thing I'm waiting for is a perfect game."

The new, more lively Haitian baseballs and the designated-hitter rule make it harder for Ryan to accomplish his mother's wish, but the thing that bothers the Express more than either of those changes is the lowering of the mound.

"There's much more effort involved in making a delivery off a low mound than coming down full force off a high one. This is not an alibi, but I think the lower mound is responsible in part for the wildness I sometimes have."

The designated-hitter rule kept Ryan in games longer, helping him complete 26 of 39 starts for three hundred and twenty-six innings, but he might have struck out 400 batters if he had been facing pitchers in the No. 9 spots of every batting order. Koufax fanned the pitchers fifty-three times in 1965, while Ryan was able to put three strikes past the designated-hitters thirty times in 1973.

Ryan does not believe the three hundred and twenty-six innings he pitched in '73 took anything out of his strong right arm. "I don't believe the high number of pitches I threw will affect me physically. There is no doubt, though, that my control needs improving. I think I can cut down on the walks and throw fewer pitches and not have so much strain," he said with a look toward the future. "I think I can get the walks down to one hundred because I've got better rhythm than I used to have. That's sixty-two people I'd be keeping off base right there."

The prospect of an even better Ryan must be frightening to both American League batters and the people who revise the record books. But there is one strikeout mark Ryan isn't likely to approach. That was set by Matthew A. Kilroy of Baltimore in 1886. He struck out 505 batters. He did it throwing from a mound only 50 feet from home plate.

"You not only couldn't hit Nolie from that distance," catcher Jeff Torborg yelps, "a catcher couldn't possibly handle his pitches. I have enough trouble when he's throwing from 60 feet, 6 inches. And the umpires," he adds, "would have to have very good ears, because they'd never *see* his fastball."

BOB GIBSON
STATISTICS

ROBERT GIBSON

Born November 9, 1935, at Omaha, Neb.
Height, 6.01. Weight, 193.
Throws and bats righthanded.
Attended Creighton University, Omaha, Neb.

Established major-league record, lowest earned-run average, season, 300 or more innings (1.12) 1968.
Established major-league record for most seasons, 200 or more strikeouts (9), 1970.
Tied major-league record for most strikeouts, inning (4), June 7, 1966 (fourth inning); struck out three batters on nine pitched balls, May 12, 1969 (seventh inning).
Established National League record, lowest earned-run average, season, 200 or more innings (1.12), 1968; most strikeouts, lifetime, right handed pitcher (2,786) 1972.
Tied National League record for most consecutive batters struck out, start of game (5), April 11, 1967.
Led National League in complete games with 28 in 1969.
Pitched 11-0 no-hit victory against Pittsburgh Pirates, August 14, 1971.
Tied for National League lead in shutouts with 5 in 1971.
Named National League Most Valuable Player, 1968.
Won National League Cy Young Memorial Award, 1968-70.

Year	Club	League	G	IP	W	L	Pct.	H	R	ER	SO	BB	ERA
1967—Omaha		A.A.	10	42	2	1	.667	46	26	20	25	27	4.29
1957—Columbus		Sally	8	43	4	3	.571	36	26	18	24	34	3.77
1958—Omaha		A.A.	13	87	3	4	.429	79	45	32	47	39	3.31
1958—Omaha		International	20	103	5	5	.500	88	35	28	75	54	2.45
1959—Omaha		A.A.	24	135	9	9	.500	128	59	46	98	70	3.07
1959—St. Louis		National	13	76	3	5	.375	77	48	28	48	39	3.32
1960—St. Louis		National	27	87	3	6	.333	97	61	54	69	48	5.59
1960—Rochester		International	6	41	2	3	.400	33	15	13	36	17	2.85
1961—St. Louis		National	35	211	13	12	.520	186	91	76	166	*119	3.24
1962—St. Louis		National	32	234	15	13	.536	174	84	74	208	95	2.85
1963—St. Louis		National	36	255	18	9	.667	224	110	96	204	96	3.39
1964—St. Louis		National	40	287	19	12	.613	250	106	96	245	86	3.01
1965—St. Louis		National	38	299	20	12	.625	243	110	102	270	103	3.07
1966—St. Louis		National	35	280	21	12	.636	210	90	76	225	78	2.44
1967—St. Louis		National	24	175	13	7	.650	151	62	58	147	40	2.98
1968—St. Louis†		National	34	305	22	9	.710	198	49	38	*268	62	*1.12
1969—St. Louis		National	35	314	20	13	.606	251	84	76	269	95	2.18
1970—St. Louis		National	34	294	23	7	.767	262	111	102	274	88	3.12
1971—St. Louis‡		National	31	246	16	18	.552	215	96	83	185	76	3.04

Year—Team	League	G	IP	W	L	Pct.	H	R	ER	SO	BB	ERA
1972—St. Louis	National	34	278	19	11	.633	226	83	76	208	88	2.46
1973—St. Louis§	National	25	195	12	10	.545	159	71	60	142	57	2.77
Major League Totals		473	3,586	237	151	.610	2,923	1,243	1,095	2,928	1,170	2.79

†Suffered broken leg when hit by line drive, July 15; on disabled list through Aug. 31.
‡On disabled list from May 30 to June 19.
§On disabled list from Aug. 5 to Sept. 28 due to knee surgery.
•Led league.
•Tied for league lead.

WORLD SERIES RECORD

Established following World Series records: Most consecutive games won, total Series (7); most consecutive complete games won, total Series (7); most strikeouts, game (17), October 2, 1968; most strikeouts, Series (35), 1968; most games, 10 or more strikeouts, total Series (5).

Tied following World Series records: Most games won, seven-game Series (3), 1967; most games won, no losses, seven-game Series (3), 1967; most complete games, seven-game Series (3), 1967 and 1968; most innings, one or more strikeouts, game (9), October 2, 1968.

Year	Club	League	G	IP	W	L	Pct.	H	R	ER	SO	BB	ERA
1964	St. Louis	National	3	27	2	1	.667	23	9	9	31	8	3.00
1967	St. Louis	National	3	27	3	0	1.000	14	3	3	26	5	1.00
1968	St. Louis	National	3	27	2	1	.667	18	5	5	35	4	1.67
World Series Totals			9	81	7	2	.778	55	17	17	92	17	1.89

ALL-STAR GAME RECORD

Year	League	IP	W	L	Pct.	H	R	ER	SO	BB	ERA
1962	National (2nd game)	2	0	0	.000	1	1	1	1	2	4.50
1965	National	2	0	0	.000	2	0	0	3	1	0.00
1967	National	2	0	0	.000	2	0	0	2	0	0.00
1969	National	1	0	0	.000	2	1	1	2	1	9.00
1970	National	2	0	0	.000	3	2	2	0	0	9.00
1972	National†	2	0	0	.000	1	0	0	2	1	0.00
All-Star Game Totals		11	0	0	.000	11	4	4	10	5	3.27

Member of National League All-Star team in 1962 (first game) and 1968; did not play. Named to National League All-Star team for 1966 game; replaced due to injury.
†Credited with one putout.

JIM PALMER
STATISTICS

JAMES ALVIN PALMER

Born October 15, 1945, at New York City, N. Y.
Height, 6.03. Weight, 195.
Throws and bats righthanded.
Attended Arizona State University, Tempe, Ariz., and
Towson State College, Towson, Md.

Led Northern League in wild pitches with 23 in 1964.
Pitched 8-0 no-hit victory against Duluth-Superior, June 19, 1964.
Pitched 8-0 no-hit victory against Oakland, August 13, 1969.
Tied for American League lead in shutouts with 5 and balks with 3 in 1970.
Won National League Cy Young Memorial Award, 1973.
Received reported $60,000 bonus to sign with Baltimore Orioles, 1963.

Year	Club	League	G	IP	W	L	Pct.	H	R	ER	SO	BB	ERA
1964—Aberdeen	North.		19	129	11	3	.786	75	42	36	107	*130	2.51
1965—Baltimore	American		27	92	5	4	.556	75	49	38	75	56	3.72
1966—Baltimore	American		30	208	15	10	.600	176	83	80	147	91	3.46
1967—Baltimore	American		9	49	3	1	.750	34	18	16	23	20	2.94
1967—Rochester‡	Int.		2	7	0	0	.000	12	9	6	6	5	11.57
1967—Miami	Fla. St.		5	27	1	1	.500	20	6	6	16	10	2.00
1968—Miami	Fla. St.		2	8	0	0	.000	4	2	0	5	9	0.00
1968—Rochester	Int.		2	4	0	0	.000	4	6	6	6	8	13.50
1968—Elmira†	East.		6	25	0	2	.000	18	13	12	26	19	4.32
1969—Baltimore	American		26	181	16	4	*.800	131	48	47	123	64	2.34
1970—Baltimore	American		39	*305	20	10	.667	263	98	92	199	100	2.71
1971—Baltimore	American		37	282	20	9	.690	231	94	84	184	106	2.68
1972—Baltimore	American		36	274	21	10	.677	219	73	63	184	70	2.07
1973—Baltimore	American		38	296	22	9	.703	225	86	79	158	113	2.40
Major League Totals			242	1,687	122	57	.681	1,384	549	499	1,093	620	2.71

*Led league.
†On disabled list with injured right shoulder from July 3 through August 8.
‡Recalled by Baltimore Orioles and placed on disabled list for remainder of season, August 28.
•Tied for league lead.

CHAMPIONSHIP SERIES RECORD

Year	Club	League	G	IP	W	L	Pct.	H	R	ER	SO	BB	ERA
1969	Baltimore	American	1	9	1	0	1.000	10	2	2	4	2	2.00
1970	Baltimore	American	1	9	1	0	1.000	7	1	1	12	3	1.00
1971	Baltimore	American	1	9	1	0	1.000	7	3	3	8	3	3.00
1973	Baltimore	American	3	15	1	0	1.000	11	3	3	15	8	1.80
Championship Series Totals			6	42	4	0	1.000	35	9	9	39	16	1.92

WORLD SERIES RECORD

Youngest pitcher to win complete World Series shutout game (20 years, 11 months), October 6, 1966.

Year	Club	League	G	IP	W	L	Pct.	H	R	ER	SO	BB	ERA
1966	Baltimore	American	1	9	1	0	1.000	4	0	0	6	3	0.00
1969	Baltimore	American	1	6	0	1	.000	5	4	4	5	4	6.00
1970	Baltimore	American	2	15⅔	1	0	1.000	11	8	8	9	9	4.60
1971	Baltimore	American	2	17	1	1	1.000	15	5	5	15	9	2.65
World Series Totals			6	47⅔	3	1	.750	35	17	17	35	25	3.21

ALL-STAR GAME RECORD

Year	League	IP	W	L	Pct.	H	R	ER	SO	BB	ERA
1970	American	3	0	0	.000	1	0	0	3	1	.000
1971	American	2	0	0	.000	1	0	0	2	0	.000
1972	American	3	0	0	.000	1	0	0	2	1	.000
All-Star Game Totals		8	0	0	.000	3	0	0	7	2	.000

VIDA BLUE
STATISTICS

VIDA ROCHELLE BLUE, JR.

Born July 28, 1949, at Mansfield, La.
Height, 6.00. Weight, 190.
Throws left and bats left and righthanded.
Attended Southern University, Baton Rouge, La.

Tied American League record for most strikeouts (9), consecutive plate appearances, August 18 (2), August 28 (1), September 2 (2), September 7 (1), September 11 (2), September 16 (1), 1972.
Pitched 6-0 no-hit victory against Minnesota, September 21, 1970.
Won American League Cy Young Memorial Award, 1971.
Most Valuable Player in the American League, 1971.
Led American League in shutouts with 8 in 1971.

Year	Club	League	G	IP	W	L	Pct.	H	R	ER	SO	BB	ERA
1968—Burlington	Midwest		24	152	8	*11	.421	102	67	42	*231	80	2.49
1969—Birmingham	South		15	104	10	3	.769	80	40	37	112	52	3.20
1969—Oakland	American		12	42	1	1	.500	49	34	29	24	18	6.21
1970—Iowa	A.A.		17	133	12	3	*.800	88	40	32	*165	55	2.17
1970—Oakland	American		6	39	2	0	1.000	20	12	9	35	12	2.08
1971—Oakland	American		39	312	24	8	.750	209	73	63	301	88	*1.82
1972—Oakland†	American		25	151	6	10	.375	117	55	47	111	48	2.80
1973—Oakland	American		37	264	20	9	.688	213	108	96	158	105	3.28
Major League Totals			119	808	53	28	.654	608	282	244	629	271	2.72

*Led league.
†On restricted list, March 30 through April 27, 1972.
‡Tied for league lead.

CHAMPIONSHIP SERIES RECORD

Year	Club	League	G	IP	W	L	Pct.	H	R	ER	SO	BB	ERA
1971—Oakland	American		1	7	0	1	.000	7	5	5	8	2	6.43
1972—Oakland	American		4	5⅔	0	0	.000	4	0	0	5	1	0.00
1973—Oakland	American		2	7	0	1	.000	8	8	8	3	5	10.29
Championship Series Totals			7	19⅔	0	2	.000	19	13	13	16	8	6.05

WORLD SERIES RECORD

Year	Club	League	G	IP	W	L	Pct.	H	R	ER	SO	BB	ERA
1972—Oakland		American	4	8⅔	0	1	.000	8	4	4	5	5	4.15
1973—Oakland		American	2	11	0	1	.000	10	6	6	8	3	4.91
World Series Totals			6	19⅔	0	2	.000	18	10	10	13	8	4.58

ALL-STAR GAME RECORD

Year	League	IP	W	L	Pct.	H	R	ER	SO	BB	ERA
1971	American	3	1	0	1.000	2	3	3	3	0	9.00

NOLAN RYAN
STATISTICS

LYNN NOLAN RYAN

Born January 31, 1947, Refugio, Tex.
Height, 6.02. Weight, 175.
Throws and bats righthanded.
Attended Alvin Junior College, Alvin, Tex.

Set major league record (since 1900) for strikeouts in a season with 383 in 1973, for strikeouts in consecutive seasons (1972-73) with 712, and for 10 or more strikeouts in a game 23 times in 1973.
Tied major league record for strikeouts in three consecutive games with 41 in 1973. Tied major league record by striking out side on nine pitches, April 19, 1968 (third inning) and on July 9, 1972.
Set American League records for most consecutive batters struck out (8), July 9, 1972.
Tied following American League records: most strikeouts, nine-inning night game (17), Sept. 30, 1972; strikeouts in two consecutive games (30).
Tied for Appalachian League lead in hit batsmen with 8 in 1965.
Led Western Carolinas League in games started with 28 in 1966.
Named Outstanding Pitcher in Western Carolinas League, 1966.

Year	Club	League	G	IP	W	L	Pct.	H	R	ER	SO	BB	ERA
1965—Marion		Appal.	13	78	3	6	.333	61	47	38	115	56	4.38
1966—Greenville		W. Carol.	29	183	*17	2	.895	109	59	51	*272	*127	2.51
1966—Williamsport		East.	3	19	0	1	.000	9	6	2	35	12	0.95
1966—New York		National	2	3	0	1	.000	5	5	5	6	3	15.00
1967—Winter Haven†		Fla. St.	1	4	1	0	1.000	1	1	1	5	3	2.25
1967—Jacksonville‡		International	1	7	1	0	1.000	3	1	0	18	3	0.00
1968—New York§		National	21	134	6	9	.400	93	50	46	133	75	3.09
1969—New York§		National	25	89	6	3	.667	60	38	35	92	53	3.54
1970—New York		National	27	132	7	11	.389	86	59	50	125	97	3.41
1971—New York x		National	30	152	10	14	.417	125	78	67	137	116	3.97
1972—California		American	39	284	19	16	.543	166	80	72	*329	157	2.28
1973—California		American	41	326	21	16	.567	238	113	104	383	162	2.87
American League Totals			80	610	40	32	.555	404	193	176	712	319	2.59
National League Totals			105	510	29	38	.433	369	230	208	493	344	3.58
Major League Totals			185	1,120	69	70	.496	773	423	379	1,205	663	3.04

*Led league.   †On military list through May 13.
‡Suffered elbow injury; on disabled list July 16 through August 30.
§On disabled list with blisters on pitching hand from July 30 through August 30.
xTraded with Pitcher Don Rose, Outfielder Leroy Stanton and Catcher Francisco Estrada to California Angels for Infielder Jim Fregosi, December 10, 1971.

CHAMPIONSHIP SERIES RECORD

Year	Club	League	G	IP	W	L	Pct.	H	R	ER	SO	BB	ERA
1969—New York		National	1	7	1	0	1.000	8	2	2	7	2	2.57

WORLD SERIES RECORD

Year	Club	League	G	IP	W	L	Pct.	H	R	ER	SO	BB	ERA
1969—New York		National	1	2⅔	0	0	.000	1	0	0	3	2	0.00

ALL-STAR GAME RECORD

Member of the American League All-Star Team for the 1972 game; did not play.

Year	League	IP	W	L	Pct.	H	R	ER	SO	BB	ERA
1973—	American	2	0	0	.000	2	2	2	2	2	9.00
All-Star Game Totals		2	0	0	.000	2	2	2	2	2	9.00